Wacky Rhymes

A. J. WEARME

S☀CCIONES

ISBN: 9781088865798

Published by Socciones Editoria Digitale
www.socciones.co.uk

This book is dedicated to my family and friends

Dog and Toad

My dog ran down the road
And he ran pretty fast,
He ran straight past a toad
And so, the toad came last.

Deathwatch Beetle

This morning on my windowsill
I saw a deathwatch beetle,
I tried to stay well clear of it
Its bite can be quite lethal.

The Chicken and the Hen

Today I saw a chicken
It was playing with a hen.
I thought I'd like the taste of it
So I ate it there and then.

Hyena

I've just seen a hyena
After getting out of the bath,
If he thinks that he's staying there
He must be having a laugh.

I Sleep in my Car

I sleep in my car
It's cheaper by far,
To stay in a room
Costs more I assume.

Work Late

I turn up for work late
I take longer for my break,
But I get my work done
Then go home for some fun.

Sauce in my Stew

I always put sauce in my stew
It's the obvious thing to do,
It doesn't taste too good
But it's better than the pud.

Marriage

Would you like to marry?
It's a big weight to carry!
I like to be single
So I can go out and mingle.

Man on a Tram

I once saw a very big man,
I watched him get off the tram.
We carried on going
And then without knowing,
The same man got back on the tram.

Young Man from Dundee

There was a young man from Dundee,
Who used to eat all he could see.
He went on a diet
Became very quiet
And now he talks only to me.

Roller-Coaster

I love a roller-coaster
And I'm not a boaster.
It takes you up,
Then flings you 'round
So you can make the most sir.

Public Enemy

I'm public enemy number one;
I can't do right for doing wrong.
No one likes me, I don't care
As long as I've got my full head of hair.

Write a Story

I'd like to write a story
But not claim any glory,
For having fame is very lame
And frankly it would bore me.

Hole in my Shoe

I think there's a hole in my shoe,
That gives me something to do,
I'll go to the kitchen
And fix it with stitching,
Well that and a big pot of glue.

Russell's Sprouts

Try to eat sprouts from Brussels,
They might help you grow big muscles.
They're lovely and green
To help keep you lean,
But make sure you don't pinch Russell's.

Fair play Golf

I put butter on my putter
To give it extra slip,
I also use another tool
It's called a microchip.

Mazda

I really love my Mazda
For driving down to Asda,
To buy the essentials for my team
Like fruit and veg and pasta.

Dentist

I've just been to the dentist
They really touched my senses,
I've just found out
Without a doubt;
That guy was an apprentice.

Hayley

I've been to visit Hayley
She plays the ukulele,
But I can't play
It's fair to say
I'd need to practice daily.

Gnu

Have you ever seen a gnu?
That's something I'd like to do.
I've never seen one in my neighbourhood
So perhaps I should look in the zoo.

Bed

I think I'll go to bed
And rest my weary head,
But there's a programme on TV
So I'll just watch that instead.

Rocket to the Moon

I'll take a rocket to the moon,
I won't be coming back too soon.
I'll have to go there for a year,
On second thoughts, I'll just stay here.

My Friend's Daughter

I like beer
That's quite clear.
My friend's daughter
Just drinks water.

The Question

The question is, what is the answer?
The answer is, what is the question?
The question is thrown
By someone who knows
The answer is just a suggestion.

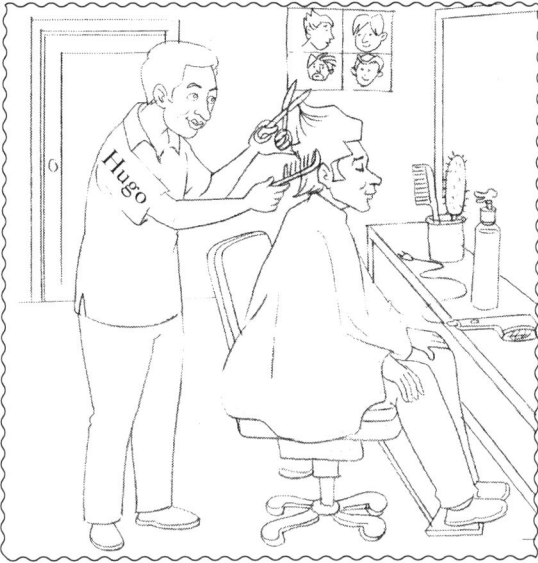

Hugo

My friend works at the barbers
He always cuts my hair,
Every time I need a trim
I ask if Hugo's there.

Cheers

Only say cheers
When you're getting the beers,
For crying out loud
Are you buying a round?

Driving Lessons

I'll teach my friend to drive
No matter what it takes,
She struggles with the pedals
So I tell her, 'Thems the brakes'.

Kentucky

I once had a friend from Kentucky
Who always thought he was lucky,
He found out one night
His instinct was right,
That's credit for being so plucky.

My Thai Friend

I met a girl from Thailand
I wore a brand-new tie,
I said, 'You speak good English
Well, it's better than my Thai'.

Onions

Some may say
I've lost the plot
'Cos I like onions
That's shallot.

Socks

You should never buy socks without trying,
For you never quite know what you're buying.
They might be too tight
To wear in the night
And that doesn't help when you're flying.

Towel Rail

My heated towel rail
Is now up for sale,
It looks like a lot
But it doesn't stay hot.

Instant Bath

I like to use deodorant
Instead of antiperspirant,
I'm not just having a laugh
But it feels like an instant bath.

Bank Statement

You work hard every month
So you think you've earnt a lot,
But then your statement tells you
Just how much you haven't got.

Walking

Walking is fun
Out there in the sun,
It's good for the ticker
But running is quicker.

They Said it was Easy

They said it was easy
And plop,
So that's how I knew
When to stop.

Thirsty on Thursdays

I always feel thirsty on Thursdays
I haven't quite figured out why,
It might be 'cos drinks are only half-price
If you get to the bar before five.

Have you ever tried to Yodel?

Have you ever tried to yodel?
I really think you should,
I do it with a ladle
But it doesn't sound too good.

Heel-Toe

Why not try to walk heel-toe?
It's quite the safest way to go.
You never know; if you're a chancer
It might make you a better dancer.

Bionic Tonic

I like a drink of tonic,
It might sound quite ironic.
But just one sip
On my top lip
Can make me feel bionic.

Curtains

I like curtains
That's for certain,
As you can see
It's curtains for me.

Eat Healthy

Cut out salt and sugar
They told us at the joint,
I guess I really should take heed
But what would be the point?

Shaving

Shaving daily
Drives me crazy,
I use balm
To keep me calm.

Cricket

Cricket is a game
Where the bowling can cause doubt,
If you get a googly
Just make sure you're not caught out.

Ride your Bike

Ride your bike
If you like,
Up and down
Into town.

Wear your helmet
Don't be lazy,
Leaving it
Would just be crazy.

Don't forget
Your handlebars,
They're on there
To steer 'round cars.

I love my bike
I think it's great,
And best of all;
No number plate.

My Friend Bill

If you go into town one day
You might meet my friend Bill,
He lives in a house, it's a very nice house
On top of a very big hill.

Pigeon Pie

A bird flew through my window
It gave me quite a fright,
But then I had a great idea,
It's pigeon pie tonight!

Snakes

I'm not keen on snakes
Especially the adder,
To tell you the truth
I'd prefer a subtractor.

Snooker

Snooker's my game,
You may feel the same.
And I like to knock it,
Straight into the pocket.

Bad Camping

If there is one thing
That I'd like to prevent,
It has to be loitering
Within a tent.

Chocolate Clock

When you're in the mood
For a cup of hot choc,
Get that hot choc
Straight from the clock.

Tall Paula

I have a friend called Paula,
I think I'll go and call her,
She says we could be quite close
If I was two feet taller.

Trainee

I'm training a trainee
To drive a brand-new train,
And once he's been trained
I can train someone again.

Valentine's Day

I like to do things
Which are good for my health,
Like on Valentine's day
Send a card to myself.

Waving

You should always wave
When you're on a boat,
'Cos that's what keeps
The boat afloat.

Rhyming

When I've finished rhyming
I usually want more,
It's always a pleasure
And never a chore.

Reflection

I'd like to meet a pretty girl
Who I could take for dinner,
The ugly mug I always see
Stares straight back from the mirror.

My Noisy Dog

I've bought a brand-new pet
But no one likes him yet,
I say he's alright;
His bark's worse than his bite.

Rhyming Slang

You should never pay more than ten pence,
For a verse that just doesn't make sense.
It shouldn't need rhyme
Or plenty of time,
But at least you should know what it meant.

Shampoo

Don't get shampoo in your eye,
I'm sure I don't need to say why.
That stuff really stings
If you haven't got wings
And you can't find a safe place to fly.

Camel's Tooth

Today when I was at the zoo
I saw a massive camel,
Its teeth were looking very good
Especially the enamel.

My Neighbour

I'm off to see my neighbour
I go there every year,
I must say that I like her
'Cos she gives me lots of beer.

Quilts

I've started a business
Making big quilts,
I sold my first one
To a woman on stilts.

Finale

So here's my final daft ditty,
I hope you found the book witty.
Perhaps I'll write again someday
Or win the lotto, who can say?

Printed in Great Britain
by Amazon